Puppy Breath

Pat Trant Kidd

Illustrated by T. D. Roebuck

To order additional copies of this book, contact:
Xlibris Corporation
1-888-795-4274
www.Xlibris.com
Orders@Xlibris.com

This book is dedicated to:

My Children:

Kimberly K. Maddox
Lex L. Kidd
Trant L. Kidd

My Grandchildren:

Tommy Lee Fuller
Patrick L. Fuller
Kathryn E. Maddox
Karson L. Kidd
Kelsey L. Kidd
Kalum S. Kidd
Elizabeth L. Kidd
Cameron Kidd
Lex L. Kidd

Great Grandchildren:

Samantha K. Fuller
Kyndel L. Fuller
Thomas A. Fuller

The greatest and most beautiful things in the world
are neither seen nor heard but are felt in the
heart. God bless all children.

I am a puppy, a very *special* puppy. I am a black and brown rottweiler. My name is Boudreaux. I belong to special children. Today I could *not* take a nap because the children were *not* making noise.

The television sets were *not* turned on, computer games were not being played, the bath tub was not running over with water, and the cat's hair was *not* being secretly cut behind the sofa.

Silence such as this—no noise, no sounds, and no sleep—added up to *equal no children,* and this bothered me.

I got up and shook my head several times, opened my eyes, and saw a wonderful surprise. Towering above me was a real live spruce tree that belonged outside. Only the children would bring a tree that belonged outside, inside.

It was decorated
with colored balls, bells,
and lights that winked
and blinked.

Beneath the tree were packages wrapped
with red, green, and gold bows. The entire
room was covered with wrapping paper,
tape, scissors, sacks, and a bottle of glue.
I was busy sniffing and pawing at all the
different-sized packages, trying to see
if the children had a present for me.

Just looking at all this clutter gave me a terrific idea. I thought about what I could give the children for Christmas. I wanted it to be special because I am special. It had to come from my heart. I looked around at the clutter on the floor and saw three Christmas sacks lying side by side.

Then I found the glue.
So I pressed my paw into
the glue and stamped each
sack with my paw print.

Then I blew my *breath* into each sack and placed the sacks under the tree. The next morning, the children were up early. I watched them as they went straight to my puppy print sacks.

As they opened the sacks,
much to my surprise,
hundreds of puppy bubbles
came floating out with images
like me in every bubble.
I was everywhere!
I was sitting, standing,
doing flips, and floating
over their heads.

They were so happy chasing me around the room—laughing, giggling, clapping their hands, and trying to catch me. They were making so much noise that I decided to finally take my nap. I walked around my bed once or twice. That is the usual thing for me to do. And as I stopped and looked around, I saw myself *everywhere.* I was as happy as I could be. I had given the children a special part of me *my puppy breath.*

Boudreaux—grown up - checking in
for his annual physical.
When Boudreaux talks,
his doctor listens.

Boudreaux—grown up - chewing on raw-hide bone one of his favorite positions to chew.

www.ingramcontent.com/pod-product-compliance
Lightning Source LLC
Chambersburg PA
CBHW060818290526

45792CB00005BB/1704